What Do You Think?

Is Modern Art Really Art?

Kelley Bieringer

Heinemann Library
Chicago, Illinois

© 2008 Heinemann Library
a division of Reed Elsevier Inc.
100 N. LaSalle, Suite 1200, Chicago, Illinois

Customer Service 888-454-2279
Visit our website at www.heinemannraintree.com

Editorial: Andrew Farrow and Rebecca Vickers
Design: Steve Mead and Q2A Solutions
Picture Research: Melissa Allison
Production: Alison Parsons

Originated by Chroma Graphics Pte. Ltd.
Printed and bound in China by Leo Paper Group

12 11 10 09 08
10 9 8 7 6 5 4 3 2 1

ISBN: 978-1-4329-0356-5 (hardback)

Library of Congress Cataloging-in-Publication Data
Bieringer, Kelley.
   Is modern art really art? / Kelley Bieringer.
      p. cm. -- (What do you think?)
   Includes bibliographical references and index.
   ISBN-13: 978-1-4329-0356-5 (hardback : alk. paper) 1. Art
appreciation--Juvenile literature. 2. Art, Modern--Juvenile literature.
I. Title.
   N7440.B48 2008
   709.04--dc22
                              2007016808

Acknowledgments
The author and publishers are grateful to the following for permission to reproduce copyright material:

©ADAGP, Paris and DACS, London 2007. Photo: ©2004 The Philadelphia Museum of Art/Art Resource/Scala, Florence p. 9; ©ARS, NY and DACS, London 2007. Photo: San Francisco Museum of Modern Art p. 24; ©ARS, NY and DACS, London 2007. Photo: Bridgeman Art Library p. 22; ©Bowness, Hepworth Estate. Photo: The Bridgeman Art Library/Art Institute of Chicago, IL, USA p. 11; ©Bruce Gray p. 34; ©Christia Forest pp. 37 (top), 39; ©Claes Oldenburg and Coosje van Bruggen. Photo: Collection Walker Art Center, Minneapolis. Gift of Frederick R. Weisman in honor of his parents, William and Mary Weisman, 1988 p. 48; ©Claes Oldenburg. Hirshhorn Museum and Sculpture Garden, Smithsonian Institution, Joseph H. Hirshhorn Purchase and Bequest Funds, 1994. Photographer: Lee Stalsworth p. 36 (top); Image: ©Corbis/Albright-Knox Art Gallery. Artwork: ©Pollock-Krasner Foundation/Artists Rights Society (ARS), New York p. 26; Corbis/©Andy Warhol Foundation/©The Andy Warhol Foundation for the Visual Arts p. 32; ©ARS, NY and DACS, London 2007. Photo: ©Corbis KIPA/Lefranc David p. 25; ©Corbis/Gianni Dagli Orti p. 12; Used by permission of the artists: Steve Badanes, Will Martin, and Ross Whitehead. Photo: ©Corbis/Wolfgang Kaehler p. 42; Photo by Craig Smith, compliments of the city of Tempe p. 46; Reproduced by permission of the Henry Moore Foundation. Photo: ©Corbis/Farrell Grehan p. 45; ©Damien Hirst. Photo: Stephen White. Courtesy Jay Jopling/White Cube (London) p. 28; istockphoto.com/Adam Kazmierski p. 44; ©Museum of Modern Art, New York, USA/The Bridgeman Art Library p. 14; Printed by permission of the Norman Rockwell Family Agency. Copyright ©1962 the Norman Rockwell Family Entities Photo courtesy Archives of the American Illustrators Gallery NYC, www.americanillustrators.com ©Copyright 2007 National Museum of American Illustration, Newport 02840, www.americanillutration.org p. 27; ©2006 PhotoEdit, Inc/Cindy Charles p. 50; ©Salvador Dali, Gala-Salvador Dali Foundation, DACS, London. Photo: Corbis/Bettmann©Salvador Dali, Gala-Salvador Dali Foundation/Artists Rights Society (ARS), New York p. 7; Scala Archives/©2007, Digital image, The Museum of Modern Art, New York p. 15; ©Succession Marcel Duchamp/ADAGP, Paris and DACS, London 2007. Photo: The Bridgeman Art Library/©The Israel Museum, Jerusalem, Israel/ Vera & Arturo Schwarz Collection of Dada and Surrealist Art p. 31; ©Succession Miro/ADAGP, Paris and DACS, London 2007. Photo: Corbis/Albright-Knox Art Gallery/Successió Miró p. 4; ©Succession Miro/ADAGP, Paris and DACS, London 2007. Scala Archives/©2007, Digital image, The Museum of Modern Art, New York p. 37 (bottom); ©Succession Picasso/ DACS, London 2007. Photo: Corbis/Bettmann p. 16; ©Succession Picasso/DACS 2007. Helen Birch Bartlett Memorial Collection, 1926.253, The Art Institute of Chicago. Photography ©The Art Institute of Chicago p. 19; ©Succession Picasso/ DACS 2007. Corbis/Archivo Iconografico, S.A./©Succession Picasso p. 18; ©Succession Picasso/DACS 2007. Photo: Corbis/ Francis G. Mayer/©Succession Picasso p. 21; ©Zayra Favares pp. 36 (bottom), 38; Gift of Frederick R. Weisman in honor of his parents, William and Mary Weisman, 1988 p48.

Cover photograph: Cover image of Broken Family reproduced with permission of ©Anthony Heywood. Frame by ©Getty Images/PhotoDisc

The publishers would like to thank Dr. Philip Koomen for his comments in the preparation of this title.

Table of Contents

Some words are shown in bold, **like this**. You can find out what they mean by looking in the Glossary.

> *The Harlequin's Carnival,* 1924-25
Joan Miró
Albright-Knox Art Gallery, Buffalo, New York

This example of modern art is a Surrealist painting.
Surrealist artists take reality and represent it in a
very unreal, dream-like way.

What Is Modern Art?

Many people think that good art is easy to find. That is true when one is looking at realistic paintings, like Leonardo Da Vinci's famous painting the *Mona Lisa* (see page 12). But, when it comes to the style of art called "modern art," like *The Harlequin's Carnival* (shown left), or piles of bricks and trash bags being presented as art, things get very tricky. Lots of people look at these paintings and sculptures and think that the artists have no talent. They say the artists are trying to hide the fact that they cannot make things look realistic, or that anyone could paint and sculpt like that.

What makes art good?

But many people do not agree with this opinion. They say that modern art styles are used by artists to represent the real world in very different ways. It is not possible to judge all art by how realistic it looks, because many pieces are not meant to look realistic. People have been arguing about modern art for many years. It is a never-ending discussion. Have you ever thought about modern art before, and what factors make a work of art good? Is all modern art really art? This book will help you join in that debate.

Opinions

Modern artists have enjoyed the fuss and debates they have caused. This meant that people were discussing art deeply and actually taking the time to look at it. The debate about modern art, which began over 100 years ago, is still going on today. People have learned how to support their opinions by using facts and make strong cases for and against the artistic merit of works of modern art.

Supporting an opinion

Everyone has opinions. But without factual support, an opinion is nothing more than what one person thinks. Facts that cannot be argued with provide the support that makes an opinion stronger.

There are three steps to make a supported opinion. A supported opinion is also called an argument. First, state your opinion, or *assertion*. Second, give a *reason* why your opinion is correct. Third, provide *evidence*, preferably a fact. You can remember how to do this by using the simple word **ARE**, the letters of which stand for **a**ssertion (opinion), **r**easoning, and **e**vidence.

When it comes to art, different opinions can be formed about the same piece of art *and* both can be correct. When you use facts (the evidence step) to support an opinion, then it becomes more valid. But, remember to leave yourself out of the argument. As soon as you put "I" in the sentence then it is *you* who is right or wrong, not the opinion. Instead of saying, "I think this painting is great," say, "This painting is great." You remove yourself so that the discussion is only about the artwork.

Two opposing supported opinions

Below are two opposite opinions about the same painting, supported using the three ARE steps. Can you see the assertion, the reasoning, and the evidence?

1. *Persistence of Memory* by Salvador Dali is art.
2. It is a wonderful painting of a dream world.
3. Everything is painted with great skill and attention to detail.

1. *Persistence of Memory* by Salvador Dali is not art.
2. It is made up of items that make no sense.
3. Pocket watches do not melt, and no one can tell what the thing on the ground is.

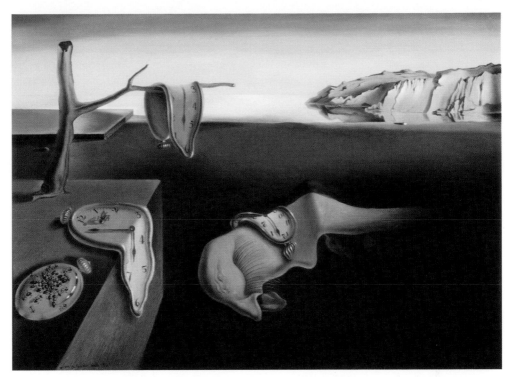

> *Persistence of Memory,* 1931, Salvador Dali, Museum of Modern Art, New York

Surrealist artist Salvador Dali (1904–1989) liked to take realistic objects and put them in dream-like settings to make people think about what they were seeing. Surrealism also expressed itself in other art forms, such as literature, movies, and the theater. The word "surreal" is still used as a description for anything that is strange, bizarre, or unexplainable.

Recognizing bias

As you think about modern art, use all your skills in critical thinking, setting aside preconceived (already formed) opinions. When you examine other people's views, consider questions such as these:

- Is this information **biased**? Does the writer have any reason to present the material in favor of one particular way of looking at things? Are proper, supported reasons given?

- Does the writer make unsupported assumptions? Are facts taken for granted rather than being supported by evidence?

- Does the writer give the sources for his or her material? If so, are the sources reliable and unbiased?

Being a critical thinker does not mean doubting or ignoring all of the views of other people. It does mean understanding the differences between personal opinion, supported opinions, and provable facts.

Analyzing art

The Harlequin's Carnival on page 4 is an excellent example to use in the debate about modern art. First, it does not look like anything that is seen in real life. On the other hand, there is a fun, busy-ness that makes it interesting. Second, the shapes are just a bunch of scribble creatures that a child could make. However, the shapes look good together because of the neatness and repeating colors. Third, the title is weird. Who or what is a **harlequin**? But, everyone knows what a carnival is, and this painting shows the controlled chaos that makes a carnival fun. Each of these ideas can be broken down into questions to help you look at this artwork.

- What does the painting look like? It looks like a crazy party.
- Do any words in the title need to be defined? Carnival is a well-known word. Harlequin means a buffoon, clown, or a person who amuses others by ridiculous behavior.
- Does the title help you understand it? It means that this is a painting of a harlequin putting on a carnival.
- What is the setting? It takes place in a room with a wall, floor, and window.
- How much skill did it take to make this? It is definitely painted neatly. People will have different opinions about the other skills.
- Do the colors have any effect on the painting? Here, the bright reds, yellows, and blues, against the black and white, add to the energy of the room.
- What material was used to make it? Paint was used. (In other artworks, especially sculptures, the material is more important.)

Can you use these seven questions to help you understand Brancusi's sculpture shown on the right? Can you write a supported opinion about it? Remember to use the three ARE steps.

How to refer to artwork when writing

✔ State the title of the piece and underline it, if writing, and make it italic if typing, for example, ***Bird in Space***.

✔ Write the artist's full name or just the last name, for example, by Brancusi.

The sentence would start like this: "***Bird in Space*** by Brancusi is a wonderful sculpture …"

> *Bird in Space,* 1923
Constantin Brancusi
Metropolitan Museum of Art, New York
Bequest of Florene M. Schoenborn, 1995

Brancusi used as little detail as possible to represent a bird.
This is one of a series of sculptures he called *Bird in Space*.

Facts versus opinions

How did modern artists decide how to show their subjects? Most modern artists took the basic **elements**, parts of the subject, and put them together in a new way in two different types of art: two-dimensional and three-dimensional art. Two-dimensional art is flat, like a drawing or painting. It has height and width, but no depth. Three-dimensional art has height, width, and depth. One can look at it from different angles, front and back.

Barbara Hepworth's *Two Figures (Menhirs)*, shown right, is a three-dimensional example of the basic elements of her subject, in this case the artist's vision of **menhirs**, the prehistoric standing stones found throughout the world. As well as representing the menhirs in wood rather than stone, by entitling the work *Two Figures*, Hepworth has added her opinion that the large stones put in place by our ancestors are like giants striding across the landscape. Let's use *Two Figures (Menhirs)* to look at the difference between a fact and an opinion. Many people forget that their opinions are not facts. It is vital to know the difference when constructing an argument. Here are some facts about this piece:

- The sculpture is made up of two wooden forms.
- One is larger than the other.
- The two pieces are mounted on a wooden base.
- The two wooden forms have had shapes carved into and through them.
- The insides surfaces of the shapes are painted white.

Now let's look at some opinions:

- The two wooden forms look like human figures.
- They represent prehistoric standing stones.
- They are stuck into the wood base like menhirs are stuck into the ground.

See if you can use any of the facts to support the opinions.

Now that you have learned something about modern art and how to look at it, try to form a supported opinion about *Two Figures (Menhirs)*. First try to answer the seven questions on page 8. The answers you come up with should help you start to form an opinion about the artwork. Referring to the box on page 8 and your answers to the seven questions, write a supported opinion about this sculpture. Find a classmate who disagrees with you and see if one of you can change the other's mind. There is nothing wrong with changing your opinion about art as you learn more about it. In fact, many people find that a piece of art they disliked at first becomes one of their favorites.

Understanding the captions beneath artwork

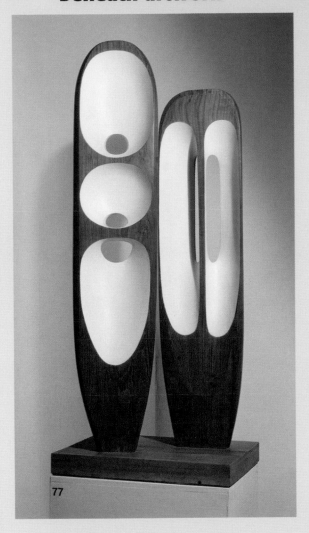

77

When a work of art is shown in a book, there is a caption that gives information about the work.

✔ The top line gives the title and date of the artwork. Sometimes, as here, there is more than one year given. This means that the artist worked on the piece during more that one year. The **medium** (what it is made of) can also be provided. In some cases the measurements of the artwork may be listed.

✔ The next line gives the artist's name and may also give his or her dates and country of origin.

✔ The following line tells the viewer where the piece of art can be seen or, if it is privately owned, whose collection it belongs to.

Labels with similar information are usually provided next to or near a work of art in the place where it is exhibited.

> *Two Figures (Menhirs)*, 1954–55 (polished and painted teak wood)
> Barbara Hepworth (1903–1975), English
> Art Institute of Chicago, Chicago, Illinois

> *Mona Lisa,* 1503–1506
Leonardo Da Vinci
Louvre, Paris

The *Mona Lisa* is a classic **portrait** painting that is recognized throughout the world. It is painted in a realistic way, showing its subject as the people who knew her would have seen her. How did modern art develop from its traditional art roots?

How Did Modern Art Develop?

Art has existed since humans realized they could make marks on the walls of caves with the tips of burnt sticks. Sculptures were made from clay, metals, wood, and any other material people could find. Drawings were done with charcoal and pencil. Until the late 1700s, artists were appreciated for their ability to paint and sculpt things realistically. The closer to the real thing an artwork looked, the more talented the artist was thought to be.

But by the late 1800s, many artists in all mediums felt that the old, traditional ways were repetitive. Most of them had been trained to paint people, animals, or landscapes exactly how they looked in real life. These painters and sculptors became bored with representing what was already so recognizable. Some believed that a new invention, photography, could do it better. Instead, they set out to produce art that looked at things in a way that no one had tried before. They wanted to focus on the basic features or feel of something and use those aspects to represent it. This is how the modern art revolution began.

Looking at modern art

Richard Diebenkorn's *Ocean Park 115* is an example of an artist taking the basic elements of a landscape and redesigning them. In it, he takes the elements of a beachside, but then does not paint exactly what he sees. The large light blue square that takes up most of the painting is the ocean. What do you think the green and tan colors represent? Are they the sand and grass near the water? Diebenkorn's painting is intended to capture the simple colors and feeling of Southern California's beaches, without actually painting a beach scene. Modern artists, like Diebenkorn, also want to express emotions by using color, shapes, and lines. Sometimes, they just create a piece that is interesting to look at, even if the viewer cannot identify anything specific being represented in it, like *Lavender Mist: Number 1* by Jackson Pollock (page 22).

Of course, many artists earlier on in the story of modern art were not quite this **radical**. They still painted recognizably, but their pictures were only representations of reality, not a snapshot of what they saw. Take a look at Vincent Van Gogh's *The Starry Night*. It is obviously a picture of a town in a valley at night with the stars in the sky. However, there is nowhere in the world where the sky would look like this. The starry night that Van Gogh painted was what the real scene inspired in his imagination. These founders of modern art broke all the existing art rules to create their own imaginative representations of reality. Unfortunately, Van Gogh and many of the other groundbreaking modern artists of his time were not recognized as great until long after their deaths.

> *The Starry Night,* 1889
> Vincent Van Gogh
> Museum of Modern
> Art, New York
>
> **Van Gogh was one of the founders of what we now call modern art.**

> *Ocean Park 115,* 1979
Richard Diebenkorn
Museum of Modern Art,
New York

This painting is an example of abstract art that has no features that are immediately recognizable to the viewer.

 What should we look for in art?

Art can be described as "the creation of works of beauty or other special significance," or "imaginative skill used to represent the world around us or parts of our imagination." Which of these things do you think are important in art?

- ✔ Skillful technique
- ✔ Beauty
- ✔ Humor
- ✔ Imagination
- ✔ Originality

- ✔ Color, shape, pattern, and texture
- ✔ Something that most people could not create
- ✔ Makes people think
- ✔ Makes you feel a strong emotion

Are there any other things you think should be added to this list?

> *Picasso in his studio*

Picasso used many mediums in his artistic career.
Here he is shown creating a ceramic work.

Is Picasso's Art Really Art?

"I wanted to be a painter, and I became Picasso."

Pablo Picasso (1881–1973)

As a young boy, Pablo Picasso's talent was obvious. Art classes were always a part of his education. Traditional styles were taught, starting with basic geometric shapes, like squares and circles, which were then applied to realistic objects like landscapes and people. At the time, it was very important to draw and paint realistically.

Until he was 17, Picasso spent many hours copying the works of old masters in order to learn different techniques. In 1897 when he was 16, he entered his painting *Science and Charity* (page 18) into a well-known judged exhibition. Here, and at another exhibition, it won awards. But, Picasso was bored. He found little pleasure in painting what could be seen with anyone's eyes. In 1898 he dropped out of school, much to the anger and disappointment of his parents, who then refused to support him any more. So, he did a variety of painting and art-related jobs and barely earned a living. How did this young, almost penniless man who could paint realistically change the art world so drastically by dramatically changing his style?

The "Blue Period"

On his own for the first time in his life, Picasso started off riding high on the achievements of his paintings like *Science and Charity*. He was able to get a variety of art-related jobs, and even tried to start an art magazine with a friend, but it was unsuccessful and failed. Picasso continued to try to find unusual ways of representing realistic scenes in his paintings. The turning point was when his good friend, Carlos Casagemas, committed suicide. This began Picasso's Blue Period, from 1901-1904, in which he mainly used blue paint and began **distorting** people, or changing the way things looked.

There is some debate about his Blue Period. Some **art historians** believe Picasso was already very short of money when he began his Blue Period, and that is why he only painted in blue, which was a cheaper paint color to buy. Others say this style was so unpopular with the public that he never made any money from his Blue Period paintings and therefore became penniless.

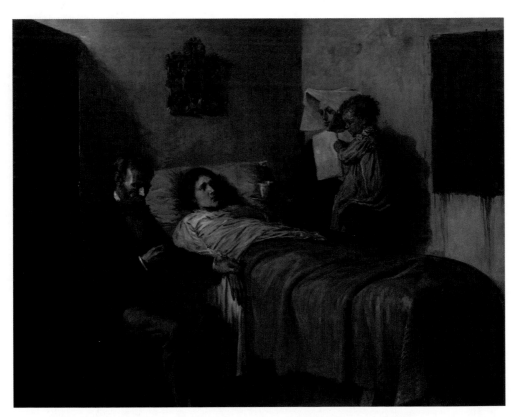

> *Science and Charity,* 1897, Pablo Picasso, Museo Picasso, Barcelona, Spain

Picasso painted this while he was still at school, and it won awards. Notice the attention to detail and use of color to create a calm atmosphere.

Either way, the Blue Period is when Picasso began to find his style as a modern artist. Traditional ways of painting did not allow him to show the depth of emotions that he felt. He distorted people by making them have unusually long body parts, like the legs and fingers in *The Old Guitarist*. Even the neck is stretched in an unnatural way making him look uncomfortable. The blue gives the painting a sad feeling of despair, and the uncomfortable bends in the guitarist's joints, such as his wrist, make the viewer feel uncomfortable as well.

> *The Old Guitarist,*
> 1903–04
> Pablo Picasso
> Art Institute of Chicago,
> Chicago, Illinois

What is now called Picasso's Blue Period contained works painted mostly in blue. They usually had sad themes that reflected his life at the time.

 What do you think makes good art?

The two paintings by Picasso shown here are very different. Look at both of them carefully. Is one better than the other? Why or why not? What reasons and evidence can you use to support your opinion?

Picasso and Cubism

Color plays a big role in Picasso's art. In his Blue Period he mainly used one color, while his next stylistic phase, **Cubism**, used color in every way. Picasso explored Cubism from 1907-1914, during which time he did nothing but try new viewpoints and color combinations. The subject of the painting was broken down, analyzed, and then put back together showing all the different angles at one time. His work at this time, along with that of his friend Georges Braque, created the Cubist art movement.

Weeping Woman, on page 21, is Cubist, although painted later than Picasso's main Cubist period. In this painting, you can see a woman who is very upset. Picasso chose to use the Cubist style to show how her emotions are jarring her from all different directions. That's why her face is broken into different shapes and colors, to show her broken emotions. Even though she is facing to one side, known as a **profile**, both sides of her face can be seen. Only one eye should be showing, but they are both there. This is how a painting in the Cubist style breaks down the subject matter and puts it back together.

Picasso and ceramics

Diversity of style and materials is another common theme within Picasso's work. In the late 1940s and 1950s, Picasso began to focus on three-dimensional forms. After working with many materials, he finally chose ceramics. Ceramics, hollow clay sculptures, and plates opened a new area of artistic expression.

But no matter what medium he worked in, exploration, color, and distortion are three elements that are always present in Picasso's work. Throughout his life he developed as an artist by using a wide variety of materials and subject matter. As the most well-known and talked about of the **pioneering** modern artists, Picasso caused many people to change their definitions of what was art and accept new ways of looking at things.

 Is Picasso's *Weeping Woman* really art?

According to one art student, Anthony (aged 13), "This isn't art. It looks like someone scribbled to draw a really bad face. The nose isn't even in the right place; it's in the middle of her cheek." But many art critics think this is a great example of how art and life mix to make great works of art. What do you think?

> *Weeping Woman,* 1937
Pablo Picasso
Tate Modern, London

This is one of Picasso's most widely known paintings. It is painted in the Cubist style. This expression of modern art ignored traditional perspective and often showed things from more than one viewpoint or angle in the same painting.

> *Lavender Mist: Number 1,* 1950
Jackson Pollock
National Gallery of Art, Washington, D.C.

Many people love the hidden images they think they
see within the paint splatters, while others think this
picture shows that Jackson Pollock had no talent.

Jackson Pollock: Process Versus Product

J ackson Pollock (1912–1956) was born and raised in the United States. As an artist in the early to mid-1900s, he was thought to be **avant-garde**. Avant-garde art is considered to be ahead of its time and usually opposes accepted ideas and traditions. Often it needs to be explained for the viewer to understand it, which makes avant-garde artwork hard for many people to enjoy.

Lavender Mist: Number 1 is one of Jackson Pollock's better-known and appreciated paintings. But paintings like *Guardians of the Secret* (page 24), are what caught the art world's attention. However, in all of Pollock's most celebrated works, the process is apparent. Huge canvases would be laid out on the floor. Pollock would walk around and on them as he dripped paint, sand, and broken glass. In 1947 he said, "On the floor I am more at ease, I feel nearer, more a part of the painting, since this way I can walk around in it, work from all four sides and be literally 'in' the painting." This way of painting broke every rule in the art world. Was it the way he painted or what the paintings looked like that caught everyone's attention? Were Jackson Pollock's paintings really art?

Mystery and simplicity

In paintings like *Guardians of the Secret*, Pollock used many mysterious symbols. It is hard to tell if the figures in this painting are male or female. There appears to be writing that cannot be read. These mysteries pull viewers in as they try to understand what secret is being guarded. On the other hand, because everything is unknown, it is very hard to relate to. People may prefer the more simplistic *Lavender Mist: Number 1*. These examples of Pollock's paintings show how his inventive techniques interested the avant-garde art world and, eventually, the general public.

> *Guardians of the Secret,* 1943
Jackson Pollock
San Francisco Museum of Modern Art, San Francisco, California

This type of art, usually known as **abstract expressionism**, was particularly loved by a trendy and slightly snobby crowd. In many ways, they enjoyed the fact that few people claimed to understand or appreciate Pollock.

Style or content?

Pollock's painting style fascinated many people. Most of his canvases were at least three times bigger than he was. Working on such a big canvas intimidates most artists, but not Pollock. It was an athletic adventure, stretching every muscle to the fullest. Some thought he was just pushing the boundaries of what was acceptable.

To Pollock, however, his method of "action painting," as it came to be called, allowed him to be "in" the painting, and created a work of intense personal meaning. In 1947, he said, "When I am in my painting, I'm not aware of what I'm doing. It is only after a sort of 'get acquainted' period that I see what I have been about. I have no fears about making changes, destroying the image, etc. because the painting has a life of its own. I try to let it come through. It is only when I lose contact with the painting that the result is a mess. Otherwise there is pure harmony, an easy give and take, and the painting comes out well." Most artists would say their works have great personal meaning, but none before Pollock had dripped or splattered their paintings. Why was it such a big deal when Pollock did it? Does the process really matter? Regardless of how you feel about Pollock's work, he definitely starts conversations and makes people question their opinions about art and the processes by which art is made.

> *Pollock in his studio*

Pollock is an artist who is closely identified with his paintings. It is hard to separate the process of how he painted from the final paintings.

Imagination station

Look at Pollock's *Convergence*. What five words would you use to describe this painting? What animals do you think left these tracks? What foods might the colors represent? How would this painting feel if you touched it?

Definition of "convergence":
◆ a meeting place
◆ to come together toward a common point
◆ the occurrence of two or more things coming together

Does understanding the title help you form a better opinion about the painting? Which of the three definitions do you think Pollock was thinking of when he named the painting?

> *Convergence,* 1952
Jackson Pollock
Albright-Knox Art Gallery, Buffalo, New York

Convergence is a Pollock painting that appeals to the general public. The busy lines and bright colors spark people's imaginations.

What do you think?

Use the ARE three-step process to support three opinions that demonstrate why Pollock *was* or *was not* a great artist. You may use any of his paintings as examples, but remember to refer to them correctly (see page 8).

Painting of a painting

Norman Rockwell's *The Connoisseur* appeared on the cover of *The Saturday Evening Post* in 1962. At this time people were still forming their opinions about modern art. The stuffy man in the suit, with gloves in his hands, a hat, and a cane, represents old styles and traditions. He is seen confronting the loud, bright, busy colors of the Pollock-like painting. But, his face cannot be seen. Is he appreciating the museum or gallery's choice of this example of modern art, or does he despise it? The viewers of the magazine cover were left to decide how the man is reacting. Rockwell **depicts** the debate that has been raging over new art forms, but doesn't answer the question of whether modern art is really art.

> *The Connoisseur,* 1962
Norman Rockwell
Norman Rockwell Museum of Stockbridge, Massachusetts

"That we have come to accept the achievements of Picasso…and Jackson Pollock, does not necessarily mean that their work is either fully understood or that this acceptance is universal." From *MoMA Highlights*, 2004

Try this: Pretend you are the man in *The Connoisseur*, and write a column that will appear in tomorrow's paper reviewing Pollock's work. Make sure you give reasons and evidence as to why your assertions (opinions) are correct. (Remember – ARE.)

> *Away from the Flock,* 1994
Damien Hirst
Serpentine Gallery, London

Hirst likes to put a variety of animals and animal parts, from sharks to bull's heads, in formaldehyde. What do you think? Is putting an animal in formaldehyde really art or just a scientific process?

"That's just gross. Who wants to see a dead animal floating in anything?" **Opinion of Jolee, 28, a social worker**

Is *This* Art?

*"The artist should never try to be popular.
Rather the public should be more artistic."*

Oscar Wilde (1854-1900)

Imagine going to an art gallery or museum and seeing a dead animal almost perfectly preserved. You can look at it from all sides. Are the same thoughts going through your head and the person next to you? Probably not. Avant-garde art usually opposes accepted ideas and traditions. Also, it often requires an extra explanation to understand what is being done. Does that make more people want to look at and think about it, or only shake their heads and walk away?

One of the main things avant-garde artists like is **controversy**, a public argument between two sides with different opinions. They love the fact that people are forced to question basic ideas of what is considered to be art. They want to make sure people do not just accept what "experts" decide is art. The controversy makes people question whether or not traditional art rules are right. There is not always an answer, but the debate is fascinating.

"Readymades"

Marcel Duchamp is famous for many "readymade" pieces of art. He describes them as, "a work of art, without an artist to make it." He would find "readymades," objects that he thought could be presented as art, and then sign them as R. Mutt. In 1917 Duchamp bought a urinal and entered it into an art exhibition under the title, *Fountain*. Then, the exhibition officials discovered that R. Mutt was not a real person. So, *Fountain* was banned from the show, and the art committee wanted to know who the supposed artist was. They were shocked to find out it was the famous French Surrealist Marcel Duchamp. How could a famous artist, even a Surrealist, enter a urinal into an art show?

How did a piece like this get selected for the show in the first place? Obviously someone liked it and thought it really was art. It was the public's disgust that caused an emergency meeting where *Fountain* was banned from the show and described as immoral and unoriginal.

Strong feelings about Fountain

Most people feel very strongly about this piece. Some people, like the original committee, thought it was offensive. It was an insult to value a urinal the same way they would value a painting, like the *Mona Lisa*. Taking something out of a bathroom, where things are done in private, and putting it on public display was considered to be immoral. To top it all off, Duchamp did not even make it. He bought it and then wrote a false signature on it. Was that because he wanted people to judge *Fountain* for its artistic value without thinking about his reputation, or was it because he wanted to hide from the controversy?

On the other hand, some people like the fact that an everyday object is considered art. Things can be appreciated even though they are not created for their beauty. Some viewers even like the **irony** to be found in presenting such an object as a work of art. In this case, the irony is that Duchamp takes an item that few people would even want to touch and places it in an art show, where it is to be treasured. Regardless of how you feel about this as art, it is so widely discussed that two copies of it were made and approved by Duchamp. Which side are you on? Is this type of modern art really art?

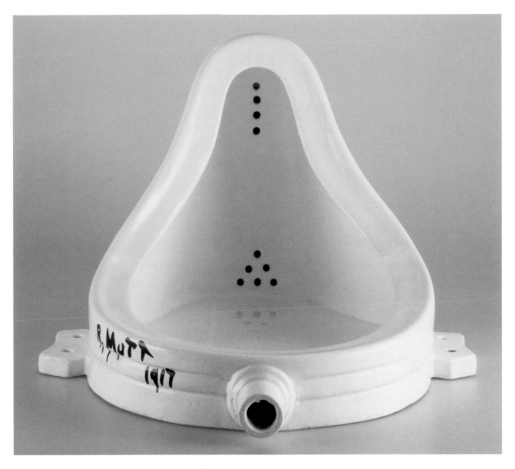

> *Fountain,* 1917 (replica)
Marcel Duchamp
Philadelphia Museum of Art, Philadelphia, Pennsylvania

Did the Surrealist artist Marcel Duchamp enter this urinal into an art show as a joke or was he serious about the artistic value of an everyday object?

 What do you think?

People go out and appreciate the beauty and artistry in nature, and can enjoy the good design in items that are intended for practical purposes. So, can people enjoy looking at an object as a work of art if it was not originally created as art?

Copy cat or artist?

Modern art is constantly being reinterpreted by artists and those who view it. Andy Warhol's *Campbell's Soup Can* is an example of **Pop Art**, which is closely related to avant-garde Art. Warhol painted a full canvas for each of Campbell's thirty-two soup flavors at that time. These paintings have been displayed individually and in groups of all sizes. Some canvases show multiple images of one can. Is it okay for an artist to take an image that already exists, use it in his or her own work, and then call it art? Warhol chose an image that every American has seen and probably eaten from.

Marcel Duchamp interpreted Warhol's motives – "If you take a Campbell's Soup can and repeat it fifty times, you are not interested in the [visual] image. What interests you is the concept that wants to put fifty Campbell's Soup cans on a canvas." It was a marketing/advertising company working for Campbell's that created the original soup can image. Warhol took it one step further. He viewed the original soup can on the shelf at the grocery store, interpreted it as an artist, and decided that it could be used to make a work of art.

> *Campbell's Soup Can (Old-fashioned Tomato Rice)*, 1962
> Andy Warhol
> Museum of Modern Art, New York

Warhol is a Pop Artist. Pop Art uses elements of popular culture, such as magazines, movies, popular music, and even bottles and cans.

Adding to or attacking art?

In recent years, someone else decided to add his interpretation to Hirst's *Away from the Flock* (see page 28).

> "Mark Bridger from Oxford poured black ink into *Away From The Flock*. Interestingly, Bridger was not protesting against the artwork, instead he claimed to be contributing to it and felt that Hirst would not object to his actions. He named the new work *Black Sheep*. He assumed Mr Hirst would not object as they were on the same creative wavelength. 'To live is to do things, I was providing an interesting addendum [addition] to his work … Art is there for creation of awareness and I added to whatever it was meant to say.' A few years later, Mr. Hirst published an art book featuring an image of the piece. When the reader pulled a tab, the tank and sheep appeared to be covered with blackness, as if ink had been poured into the container."
>
> [From *Art Crimes* December 3, 2002, http://www.renewal.org.an/artcrime]

Artist or vandal?

Art is always interpreted in some way by those that view it. First, as an artist, Hirst offended people by placing a dead animal in formaldehyde. Then, as a viewer, Bridger offended people by adding black ink to the piece, vandalizing what purported to be a work of art. Did Mark Bridger move from being a viewer to become an "artist" when he changed the original piece, or did he become a vandal, showing disrespect for the artist and his work? What do you think?

Very expensive soup

In 2006 one of Andy Warhol's 1962 soup cans, *Small Torn Campell's Soup Can (Pepper Pot)*, sold for $11.8 million. The pieces in the soup can series originally sold for $100 each!

The big cheese

American Bruce Gray is another artist who has taken an everyday object as subject. In this case, Gray made a sculpture of a wedge of cheese almost the complete opposite of a real piece of cheese. The material, color, and size were changed. Instead of a small, soft, yellow food that melts, it is large and made of hard, shiny metal. Like Hirst, Duchamp, and Warhol, Gray has taken something that everyone recognizes, given it a new twist, and called it art. Is it different from the dead sheep, the urinal, and the Campbell's Soup cans?

> *The Big Cheese #4*, recent
> Bruce Gray
> Private Collection

This sculpture is 25 inches high (63.5 cm), 29 maximum inches deep (74 cm), and 43 inches long (109 cm). It is one in a series of oversized, everyday objects inspired by the work of Pop Artist Claes Oldenburg.

Can recognizable objects be art?

Only the artist knows the purpose of his or her work, but the viewer must interpret it. The materials used are very important when dealing with recognizable objects. Everyone knows *The Big Cheese* represents a piece of cheese, even if they are not told its name. But, the purpose is very different from Duchamp's *Fountain*, which is not a traditional fountain. For many people, it is easier to enjoy *The Big Cheese* as a fun, whimsical piece, while *Fountain* makes people uncomfortable. Yet they both start with a simple, recognizable item. Does changing the original material cause this difference in attitude? What if Duchamp had made a urinal out of steel or cheese? Would it be less interesting or would it create even more controversy?

The use of recognizable objects as art often raises more questions than it answers. Many of the artists that do this want the viewers to question their basic beliefs as to what art is and what art is not. It is normal for opinions to change about art as one experiences it and learns more about it. Sometimes you will stick with your original impression, and other times your viewpoint will change. Questioning your own opinions about art will make you more able to defend what you do and don't like.

Do the materials used in the pieces of art on the last few pages take away or add value to each artwork? Can these items even be considered as works of art? What if Hirst had sewn a sheep together out of cloth and hung it in a glass case? Would that make it more artistic? Would people have taken as much notice of it?

 What do they think?

"In lots of modern or avant-garde theater you can still understand the point the writer is trying to get across. With this kind of art it's harder to understand the artist's motives."
Tom, 23, an actor

"It's not that I don't think some of this art is interesting or even funny. I just don't think it's beautiful."
Barb, 52, an office administrator

Which are professional works of art?

Which of these four pieces of art do you think were done by students and which by professional artists? The title and materials used are listed to help you.

1. *7-UP*, enamel on plaster-soaked cloth on wire

2. *Broken Heart*, tempera on paper

3. *Palm*, tempera
   on paper

4. *Person Throwing
   a Stone at a Bird*,
   oil on canvas

Answers and information

If you guessed numbers 2 and 3 are student work, you are correct!

Number 1, *7-UP*, was created by the Pop Art sculptor Claes Oldenburg (1929–) in 1961. Oldenburg came to the United States from Sweden as a child. He studied literature and drama at Yale University. After working for a few years as a newspaper reporter, he decided he wanted to be an artist. He is very well known for his enlarged versions of recognizable objects. A real can of the soft drink 7-UP is about 6 inches high (15.2 cm). Oldenburg's sculpture is 55 inches high (1.4 meters). Notice the date. It is a year before the first of Andy Warhol's *Campbell's Soup Can* paintings.

Number 2 (below), *Broken Heart*, was painted by art student Zayra Favares in tempera paints. This abstract painting represents the broken heart that everyone has had, or will have, at some time in his or her life. The shapes are fairly similar throughout the painting. Only the difference in color makes the heart visible, and it is not obvious.

Number 3 (right), *Palm*, was painted by art student Christa Forest in tempera paints. It represents the desert. The colors of the sky reflect the extreme heat. The palm tree, like every other part of the scene, is broken into its basic elements and put back together in a different way.

Number 4, *Personage Throwing a Stone at a Bird*, was painted by the Catalan artist Joan Miró (1893–1983) in 1926. This was about the same time that Constantin Brancusi made his sculpture series called *Bird in Space* (see page 9). Notice how both artists take the absolute basic elements of the person and bird, then distort them (remember distort means changing the way something looks). Brancusi stretches out the bird's body to make it the same shape as a feather. Miro takes a more fun approach by enlarging the foot and placing it beneath an almost shapeless body and circle head, with one circle eye. Both Number 1 and Number 4 represent different trends in modern art.

 What do they think?

"We have wallpaper and fabric that are just patterns of colors and shapes, and we say we like them. I don't see the difference in having art that is the same."
Stephen, 56, a company CEO

"In my class, some people who aren't very good at drawing say that their art is 'abstract' because they know that otherwise no one will understand what it's supposed to be. I think that's a kind of faking."
Julia, 13, a student

If it is thrown away, is it still art?

Several years ago an over-efficient member of the cleaning staff at a British art museum did some clearing up that made world headlines:

How auto-destructive art work got destroyed too soon

When is a bag of rubbish not a bag of rubbish? When it's an integral piece of a high-profile exhibition at one of London's most famous galleries.

Sadly, though, the distinction was lost on a cleaner at Tate Britain who chanced on the bag—part of an installation by Gustav Metzger called *Recreation of First Public Demonstration of Auto-Destructive Art*—and promptly threw it out.

The organizers of the gallery's Art and the Sixties show admitted yesterday that the bag had been mistaken for rubbish and thrown into a crusher by a cleaner on June 30. Although the bag was fished out of the Tates's crusher as soon as the mix-up came to light, Metzger is understood to have felt it was beyond rescue.

He was offered compensation, but told Tate staff that the piece was ruined and created a new bag as a replacement. the new rubbish bag is now put in a box overnight for safe keeping …

Metzger, a German artist who lives in east London, invented auto-destructive art in 1959.

According to the artist's account, the form "re-enacts the obsession with destruction, the pummelling to which individual's and masses are subjected."

He once painted hydrochloric acid on to a canvas, so that eventually the painting was entirely eaten away, in what was intended as an attack on those art dealers and collectors who manipulate modern art for profit.

[By Sam Jones from The Guardian newspaper, Friday August 27, 2004]

> Trash or art?

Gustav Metzger's installation at the gallery in London showed a transparent bag of rubbish leaning against a table leg. This picture shows a similar bag of trash in an office. Is this just trash, or could it also be art?

 What do you think?

✔ Part of the message behind Metzger's bag of trash is that all things are eventually destroyed. How much did the janitor help further this message?

✔ What makes a piece of art that is unpleasant to look at, like a bag of trash, art? Does the message behind the art as explained by the artist make it more meaningful or artistic? Can art that needs explaining really be art?

> *Fremont Troll,* 1990
Steve Badanes, Will Martin, and Ross
Whitehead (for the Fremont Art Council)
Fremont, Seattle, Washington

This sculpture is 18 feet (5.5 meters) tall and "lives"
under a bridge in the Fremont district of Seattle.
Fremont Troll makes an anti-development statement
by crushing a VW Beetle in its hand. The troll, like
the people of the city, does not want developments,
such as the freeway it lives under, to take over. This
public art is making a political statement.

Should Public Money Fund The Arts?

Many countries throughout time have used public, or government, money to pay for public art. Today public money is still used to buy and display art. It is also used to **commission** an artist to specially create a piece for a specific location, like *Fremont Troll*. This amusing sculpture "lives" in one of the driest places in a very rainy city. *Fremont Troll* is loved by people in a city where beauty is considered with every building that is added to its skyline. It was even voted as the second favorite city icon. The building known as The Space Needle (see page 44) was voted into first place.

As journalists John and Sally McDonald reported in November 2006, "Officially, the city has been adding in earnest to its collection of public art since only 1973. That's when it became one of the first cities in the country to set aside one percent of any money spent on public projects for art. Soon private businesses also were putting money into fanciful sculptures." No one has forced the city or private companies to make this financial decision. But, as a result, the city has more to offer to tourists and its residents.

Open-air art

Large Four Piece Reclining Figure by Henry Moore can be seen on the campus of Harvard University. By creating the figure in four pieces, Moore forces the viewer to see the space around the sculpture at the same time. No one can look at it and ignore the background. It becomes a part of the space it occupies, as opposed to artworks in galleries or museums. Public art forces the interaction between space and material. People are forced to include this art as they walk or drive by. This is an excellent way to bring art to those that would not otherwise be able to enjoy it.

Another way cities create beauty is by landscaping. Trees, grass, flowers, other plants and even decorative rocks are more enjoyable than concrete. But what about the cost? Landscaping is definitely more common than public sculptures, paintings, or **murals** on buildings. The **start-up costs** are definitely less than artworks, which often cost thousands of dollars. But once displayed, the artwork rarely needs anything more than an occasional cleaning. Landscaping, on the other hand, requires constant watering, trimming, and removing dead leaves. Both are thought by many people to add to the beauty of a town. Is one better than the other? Should the taxpayers be expected to pay for such things?

Most people enjoy some form of art, but many cannot afford original pieces. When it comes to outdoor art, bronzes, like *Reclining Figure*, or sculptures made of stone or metal are not cheap. The majority of people do not have the

> *Seattle, Washington skyline*

Seattle is a city that has decided that, as it gets bigger, it does not want to lose any beauty to unimaginative concrete buildings. The Space Needle (built in 1962), in the center, started this commitment to innovation.

money to buy them. But a city or state government has the money to purchase and install these types of artworks. What is the purpose of art in a city? Does everyone benefit? What if you do not like the type of modern art chosen for public display?

> *Large Four Piece Reclining Figure, 1972–73*
Henry Moore
Cambridge, Massachusetts

Some sculptures, like this figure by Henry Moore, are intended by the artists to be displayed outside. This piece, which is on the campus of Harvard University, makes a nice place to study in good weather.

 ## Public art – pro or con?

Many towns and cities do not have much in the way of public art installations. Think about a boring or neglected part of the area that you live in which could benefit from a piece of public art. Write a sample request to local officials giving your opinions on why a piece of art would enhance the area and be a good use of public money. You could even design an outdoor art piece for this space. If you don't approve of the idea of public art, try writing a mocked-up letter to the editor of your local newspaper explaining why you think such art is a waste of public resources.

Sand box with a difference

Michael Anderson's *Adornment* is an example of public art. The city of Tempe, Arizona took a park with a purpose and gave it an artistic facelift. These steel, flagstone, and concrete pieces are supposed to represent something. Think about the title. Can you guess what they are representing? Jewelry! The artist wanted this area of the park to look like the inside of a jewelry box from above. The circle leaning against the wall is either a bracelet or an earring, with a matching one in the background. The concrete walkway looks like a chain necklace with a pendant-shape and three stone seats. It gives people a place to sit and enjoy the nice weather or watch their kids play in the sand. It makes the park more inviting. It would be interesting to know how much the "jewelry" look in this area cost to create compared with the cost of the plain wooden and concrete benches that could have been used. Was the expense worth it?

> *Adornment,* 1998
Michael Anderson
Kiwanis Park overlooking Kiwanis Lake, Tempe, Arizona

This steel, flagstone, and concrete sculpture is not only functional in its playground setting, but is also a tribute to a local jewelry artist.

Taxes for public art

In Southern California, the city of Rancho Mirage tried to pass a $430 art tax on all new homes. City officials were trying to make the city more appealing, as tourism is one of the main sources of income in the area. They thought that public art would make the city more inviting, nicer looking, and more enjoyable to walk around. Residents had mixed opinions about it. Some thought it was a wonderful idea that might even cut down on graffiti and bring large artworks to people who would not otherwise be able to enjoy them.

Others liked the idea, but thought that raising the price of a new home was a bad idea, regardless of the visual benefits. They support the idea of art, but not at their own expense. What do you think? Would you vote for or against this tax? When arguing or debating this point remember to use the three ARE steps: assertion, reasoning and evidence.

Tax breaks for public art

The Asian country of Singapore has developed another way to finance public art. Instead of directly paying for it, the government encourages companies and private donors to sponsor public art. What do the companies or individuals get for being so public spirited? Tax cuts. The PATIS program (Public Art Tax Incentive Scheme) gives tax deductions up to double the appraised value of the work of public art provided. Organizations and individuals can also "adopt" works of art and get double tax deductions for paying to maintain existing public artworks.

Support your point of view

Make a flyer to convince other people to vote the same way as you in a local public art finance election. It needs to:

✔ be easy to read

✔ be not too wordy or complicated,

✔ contain clear reasons for your point

✔ be well designed and eye catching.

The writing can be done creatively, or pictures can show what your words would say. What other methods can be used to convince people of your point of view?

> *Spoonbridge and Cherry,* 1985–1988
Claes Oldenburg and Coosje Van Bruggen
Minneapolis Sculpture Garden of the Walker Art
Center, Minneapolis, Minnesota
Gift of Frederick R. Weisman in honor of his parents, William and Mary Weisman, 1988.

This work is an example of several modern art trends. First, it represents the idea of man and nature together, with the spoon representing man and the cherry representing nature. Second, the setting contrasts this theme, with the stream, which is natural, but with the city in the background. Finally, it takes common objects and turns them into art.

What's It All About?

Modern art began in the late 1800s and its influences can still be seen today. Artists in all mediums began to explore different ways to represent reality. As with any change, this made people uncomfortable. Debates began immediately that questioned the quality of the new styles of art and whether or not they should even be considered art. Most artists just wanted to create something that had never been seen before. Distortion was the common factor. Any way in which reality could be twisted, it was. Color, shape, size, and materials were all used in a variety of ways.

As soon as a new style became more acceptable, like Vincent Van Gogh's *The Starry Night* (page 14), artists would push the boundary of creativity even farther. Surrealism took real things and put them in dream-like settings. Cubism played with shape and color. Abstract Art represented things and emotions in unrecognizable ways, or just made pieces that were nice to look at. Avant-garde art pushed the limits of what is acceptable, mainly through the use of objects as art. Pop Art took recognizable images from modern culture and used them in different ways. Each of these movements was inspired at its start by a desire to see the world differently. Over the years these artists enjoyed the controversy they caused, and often created things for shock value. It was hard for the average person to understand, which became part of the appeal.

Changing opinions

As years pass, styles of art change, building on each other to invent new creative avenues. For better or worse, modern artists changed the face of the art world, and altered what the public will accept as being art.

As you read this book, did your opinions about modern art change? It is quite common to form an opinion about a piece of art and then change it once someone else explains it differently. The phrase, "beauty is in the eye of the beholder" is certainly true when it comes to modern art. What one person sees as splatters on a canvas is mesmerizing to another who cannot look away. When those two people begin to discuss the artwork, one may change his or her mind after hearing how other people see it.

Educating yourself is the best way to make an informed decision about anything.

> Research and practice
Thorough research of a topic, good notes, and team practice makes a debate interesting and informative.

How to organize your own debate

So, is modern art really art? Have you formed your own opinion yet? And what happens next? You should plan to explain your views to other people and persuade them that you are right. The best way to do this is to organize a debate with your classmates.

There are a wide variety of ways to organize your own debate about modern art. During a debate, no matter what type, there should be a (polite) clash of opinions. Debaters should both state why they are right *and* why the other side is wrong. Make sure you use the ARE format from page 6. Also, both sides should agree on which pieces will be debated. It would be very unfair for one side to introduce an artwork that the other side has never seen.

It is sometimes best that the debaters should not be told which side of the debate they will be defending. This is for two reasons. One, they need to understand both sides, and two, this way they know how to respond to the other side's arguments. The debate topic must be a sentence, not a question. One side will agree with it and the other side, disagree. The judge or audience does not have to name one side as the winners because the purpose is to learn how to make and use supported opinions.

Debate formats

Large group debate: The group should be split in half, preferably facing each other, with the two sides being **proposition** and **opposition**. Do not decide who is on which side until right before the debate. Then, give people five minutes to organize their notes. So that everyone has a chance to speak, you can work out a system where each person gets one token and no one gets to go a second time until everyone has spoken.

Small group discussion: Debaters should break into groups of four to six. Within each group, half are proposition and half are opposition. Each person must speak at least one time. In this format, students can be expected to give three to five-minute speeches.

Quick fire debates: Same as the Small Group Discussion, except each debate should take less than eight minutes, six if each person must speak for one minute. Many topics can be covered this way, either individual art pieces or artists.

Posters can be made supporting or opposing any of the topics in any form of debate. Pictures of the artwork should be included.

Hopefully this will start you on a path to great debates about art! Is modern art really art? Whether you like it or not, your opinion matters!

Find Out More

Topics

Here are some ideas for topics for debates or discussion on modern art. You can also come up with your own.

* Modern Art Is Really Art. If this book has been read by your whole group, then all the artwork can be used in the debate. If that is overwhelming, choose three to five pieces to use as examples.
* Jackson Pollock Is A Great Artist. Any modern artist can be used here.
* Pop Art is Pointless.
* Government Should Pay For Public Art.
* Modern Art Does Not Express Emotions Better Than Traditional Art.
* *Adornment* By Michael Anderson Is Art. Any specific piece of art will work. This topic is great for the Quick Fire debate format.
* *Fountain* By Duchamps Is Disgusting and Insulting.

Books

* Barnes, Rachel. *Artists in Profile: Abstract Expressionists*. Chicago: Heinemann-Raintree, 2002
  Picasso and Pollock are included in this book in the group of artists known as abstract expressionists.
* Bee, Harriet Schoenholz. (Ed.) *MoMA Highlights*. 2nd Edition. New York: The Museum of Modern Art, 2005
  This book gives important historical and artistic information about each piece that the Museum of Modern Art owns. The reading is a little challenging, but each description is less than one page long.
* Dickins, Rosie, & Griffith, Mari. *The Usborne Introduction to ART*. New York: Usborne Publishing Ltd. 2004
  This is an easy read, with lots of pictures to take you through art from some of the first known pieces to current artists. It includes many of the artists found in this book and their impact on the art world.
* Mason, Paul. *Artists in Profile: Pop Artists.* Chicago: Heinemann-Raintree, 2002
  This book contains sections on Claes Oldenburg, Andy Warhol, and other well-known Pop Artists.

- Micklethwait, Lucy. *I Spy Shapes in Art*. London: Collins, 2004
  This book is a picture book meant for very young children, but the modern art pictures are large enough that students can use this book to show examples of art in a debate or presentation.

Websites

Art Crimes

- http://www.renewal.org.au/artcrime/
  This is a fascinating website that has a variety of real life art crimes, including those involving Marcel Duchamp's *Fountain* and Damien Hirst's *Away from the Flock*.

ArtLex Art Dictionary 2006

- http://www.artlex.com
  This amazing alphabetized resource by Michael Delahunt is easy to read and understand.

Sculpture by Bruce Gray

- http://www.brucegray.com
  This website is a collection of Gray's sculptures, including links to articles and interviews with him.

The Museum of Modern Art

- http://www.moma.org
  This shows all the pieces in the New York museum's permanent collection. It is easy to access specific artists or artworks.

Glossary

abstract	nonrepresentational, not recognizable
abstract expressionism	is difficult to define. It is a modern art movement that is usually nonrepresentational, and uses colors and textures to create meaning.
art historian	expert in the history of art and its development over time. Most art historians specialize in one particular period or movement in art.
avant-garde art	usually opposes accepted ideas and traditions, and is considered to be radically new and different
bias	unfair preference for or against someone or something
circa	(abbreviated as c.) around the time
commission	piece of art specifically ordered and paid for by an organization or collector
connoisseur	someone considered to be enough of an expert in a field to pass judgment
controversy	public argument between two sides with different opinions
Cubism	modern art movement in which all of the elements are fragmented or seen from different viewpoints
depict	show
distorting	changing the way something looks
elements	parts
harlequin	comic, clown-like character, usually masked, who dresses in a bright, diamond-patterned costume
irony	expressing a meaning that is the opposite of the normal meaning
medium	material used to make something

menhirs	also called monoliths. This is the name given to large standing stones, sometimes set in rings or lines, erected by people in prehistoric times. The prehistoric monument in England called Stonehenge is formed of menhirs.
murals	big paintings usually on internal walls or the sides of a building
opposition	individual or side that disagrees with the statement being argued in a debate or discussion
pioneering	innovating in a particular field, or first to do something
Pop Art	art that uses elements of popular culture, such as magazines, movies, popular music, and even bottles and cans
portrait	painting of a particular person
profile	a side view of a face
proposition	individual or side that agrees with the statement being argued in a debate or discussion
radical	extreme or drastic
start-up costs	finance needed to get a business or other enterprise started
Surrealism	style of art that takes reality and twists it in a strange way, such as might occur in a dream

Index